God Has Brought Us From a Mighty Long Way!

God Has Brought Us From a Mighty Long Way!

A Book That Could Have Been Written From Many Believer's Lives

By
Minister Harriet E. Edmondson

E-BookTime, LLC
Montgomery, Alabama

God Has Brought Us From A Mighty Long Way!

Copyright © 2007 by Minister Harriet E. Edmondson

"From Revolution to Revelation" Copyright © 2000 by Minister Harriet E. Edmondson

All rights reserved. No part of this book may be reproduced or transmitted in any form or by any means, electronic or mechanical, including photocopying, recording, or by any information storage and retrieval system, without permission in writing from the copyright owner.

ISBN: 978-1-59824-670-4

First Edition
Published July 2007
E-BookTime, LLC
6598 Pumpkin Road
Montgomery, AL 36108
www.e-booktime.com

Contents

Phase - I - Book One
"Broken Jars of Clay, But Still Being Used In The Master's Hands"

From Revolution to Revelation 11
To My Brothers 16
To My Sisters 18
The Trial 21
Freedom 22
Restoration of the Family God's Way 23
The Women's Retreat 28
Hallelujah Jesus Found Me! 32
What does it Mean to Be Saved? 35
The Journey Was Not Even About Us 37

Phase - II - Book Two
"Chronicles of Faith"

Foreword 63
Acknowledgements 65
Introduction 69
First Wave Assault - Physical Attack 71
Second Wave Assault - Emotional 82
Third Wave Assault - The Family 88
Fourth Wave Assault - Attack On My Very Soul 92
Book II - Conclusion 99

Phase – I – Book One

"Broken Jars of Clay, But Still Being Used In The Master's Hands"

"REVOLUTIONARY?"

REASONING?"

From Revolution to Revelation
Enlightenment and Understanding

"For God's Sake We've Got to Get More Power to the People!"

The title from that 1960s-1970s era song was a direct expression of the growing frustrations of young African Americans. You see, in the 1960's and 1970's there were many misconceptions in our Society, one of which was that most of the problems that were happening in our communities were the fault of any one particular ethnic group. The truth of the matter was that our country as a whole was experiencing extremely turbulent societal and cultural changes at a rapid-fire rate of speed. As a result of these changes, we who lived in African American communities were witnessing and experiencing the most devastating results from those changes. We saw a tremendous increase in death and violence in our communities. There was a sudden and tremendous proliferation of drugs and weapons that were finding their way into our communities, homes, and into our families. Resulting in the wounding and deaths of many of our brothers, sisters, and young children. It seemed to us that weapons and drugs were much more easily attainable and available than ever before in our communities across the country. So because we were the young adults responsible for what was going on in our communities, and because so many of our families were being victimized and not to mention the fact that our children were also being placed at greater risk, we began to examine this social phenomenon. How was this happening? What exactly was going on? The guns and drugs had to be coming into our communities somehow? We didn't grow the plants that the drugs are made from and we certainly didn't have any "Smith and Wesson" factories in our back yards! We had no ships and ports to transport drugs into our neighborhoods! We also realized that no one in our communities had a stockpile of weapons to warehouse!

We began to look at the history of African American people in America and how much death, destruction, and suffering had historically been inflicted upon us by others. We realized that because it was no longer legal to openly destroy our people that there were still insidious radical groups and elements of our society that had the desire to destroy us as a people. This evil would not be changed through legislative efforts or the well-meant altruistic promises of a few seemingly well-meaning people. So we the people took it upon ourselves to attempt to protect our children and our communities.

God Has Brought Us From A Mighty Long Way!

Many of us turned to so-called revolutionary organizations, such as "The Black Panther Party" or the "Nation of Islam". Other than their sometimes violent rhetoric, the Panthers were the first organized group of black people that seemed to be offering us legitimate answers and solutions to many of our problems. Later on we investigated the "Nation of Islam", but I never really got caught up in that organization because of their disbelief in Jesus as "The Messiah." And even before I got saved, I knew better than that! So after deciding to become actively involved in the Black Panther Party and what I discovered later were their <u>erroneous teachings</u> from the Chinese leader, Chairman Mao Tse-tung's "Red Book" I became somewhat of a community activist. I began to feed children by participating in before school "Breakfast Programs". I even spoke at a couple of public community gatherings with a rallying cry out to my brothers and sisters expressing the need for us to change our ways of thinking and living. All of this in the belief that what we were being taught would make things better for our communities. Well after all of our zeal and efforts, we came to a stark and crushing realization that the "Black Panther Party" was also nothing more than a puppet-organization formed by outsiders to dupe, confuse, and divide our communities even further. The organization itself had been set up with an infiltration of covert operatives posing as members who were solely there for information-gathering purposes about the real members of the

Party! We later found out that certain agencies actually kept profiles on every "Black Panther" member in order to help the government keep track of the organization and its activities because it was considered a subversive organization.

After those experiences I returned to my normal routine of working, parenting, and supplementing my children's education. I made certain that they were aware of the truths about the wonderful contributions made by great African American men and women throughout the history and development of America which helped to make it the greatest and most powerful nation on earth that it is today.

In 1974 I began to realize that I had a lot to say and I discovered that I had an inherent gift for writing. I also realized that there was a general misconception in society about our people that all African American men were shiftless, lazy, drug and/or alcohol addicted recidivists who weren't responsible for nor cared for their own families. There was also a strong misconception that African American women were promiscuous, irresponsible, and welfare-oriented, mothers who did not have a clue as to how to respect and/or submit to the protecting, guiding and leading of our fathers or husbands!

There were also false beliefs about our not being able to appreciate one another as sisters. It was presumed that black women were jealous of one another, still under the influence of the "light-skinned/dark-skinned slave mentality" which had been passed down through generations as a result of the famous "Willie Lynch" speech called "The Making of a Slave" delivered on the banks of the James River at Jamestown in the Colony of Virginia in 1712.

So in 1974, I decided to use the gifts (that I now know) God had given me to write poems that could possibly dispel and clarify some of these misconceptions by honoring my brothers and sisters with two poems. One is called "To My Brothers" the other is simply called "To My Sisters". Later I began to write about other social ills, and the realities of our plight as being African Americans born and raised right here in America.

This is the stage in my life when I truly realized the philosophy of "the pen being mightier than the sword!" I began to pour out my soul and the soul of my people through poems. That revelation resulted in my writings presented below:

To My Brothers

So bold and so very strong...
So right and he hardly ever wronged...

Black warrior, from whence dost thou come?...
From Ancient Africa the land of the sun...

Stolen from your motherland in bondage and in shame..
Stripped of your culture and given a new name...

Why? Brother why? Must they torment you so?...
Intent on stealing your identity, your pride, and even your life...

First they stole your sisters, then they stole your mothers, and finally even your wife...

Surely Black King, even they must know, that the time has come to let us all go!...

And I as your Queen shall stand at your side, with love in my heart and oh so much pride...

My beautiful King we have nothing to hide...

God Has Brought Us From A Mighty Long Way!

And as time shall come yet as time does go, and as all of us Brothers and Sisters do know...

That with love in our hearts, and pride in our souls, a <u>just</u> and <u>equal</u> survival is a must...

And with wisdom guiding our minds and our babies in our arms, our cause is truly <u>just</u>!

To My Sisters

Black lady, beautiful black Queen...
Yes, you are everyone's dream...

With skin so velvet, ebony, and smooth...
Proud woman, in your <u>own</u> <u>domain</u> you are so adept at ways to soothe...

You are so beautiful and so very strong...
Black Queen you've always known <u>right</u> from <u>wrong</u>...

Our womanhood has always stood for <u>class</u>...
And no other race of women could even come close to our past!... We have had to struggle to merely survive!... We have had to defend our families and even our own lives!...

Motherhood, womanhood, and sisterhood have always been ours to unfurl... For we are natural women, and have raised the children of the world...

We have <u>never</u> been given respect, even when it was due!...
Yet, none of those other women even knew how to come through...

God Has Brought Us From A Mighty Long Way!

They were overprotected and their attitudes were meek and when faced with reality they would sometimes turn to strong drink...

Many times respected though deserving they were not...
My beautiful sisters we were the ones forced into living hells to rot...

We saw our men stripped, we saw our babies whipped...
The Oppressor! Yes he came well equipped!...
And all of this taking place before our very eyes...
Yet they wonder how we could have so easily despised...

They may say that we are prejudiced or filled with hate, but Ancient African traditions would only have taught us to <u>love</u>, <u>progress</u>, and <u>create</u>...

So all that we have shown them was taught us at the Seaport's gates...

Black woman I will always love thee, because of what you aspire to be...

Because of what we mean to each other in our struggles to be free!..

For I can truly understand that which is me!...

For us the future surely holds, <u>freedom</u>, <u>equality</u>, and <u>dreams untold</u>...

My Sisters just stay <u>strong</u>, <u>brave</u>, and <u>bold</u>!...
For our race will never ever die...For we <u>truly</u> are the mothers of the earth <u>you and I</u>!...

The Trial

A Black mother crying in the night...
For she knows of her young son's plight...

A trumped-up charge for a crime <u>he</u> <u>has</u> <u>not</u> <u>done</u>...
They don't care, they just say <u>Get One</u>!...

So she carries her fears walking up the courthouse steps...
Her head hung down...for she knows what to expect...

A prosecutor speaking with his mouth full of lies...
And as he looks down upon her boy you can easily see his disguise...

There is an uncaring judge staring from unseeing eyes...
As he listens intently to a tangled web of lies...

But be encouraged Black Mother and do not despair..
For the day is coming...when they will pay their fare...

And our triumphant people with <u>shout</u> all over this land...
As you walk proud and strong with your honorable son's hand-in-hand...

Written under the <u>Pen</u> <u>Name</u> "Sister Luv" - 1974

<u>Freedom</u>

Freedom, freedom at long last...

Never again ensnared by my past...

Loving my Savior for who He is...

Desiring one thing, for Him I live...

Never to forget the price He paid for me...

Jesus is the reason I am truly, truly Free...!

October 1996 - Pen Name Sister Luv

THE SKITS

Restoration of the Family God's Way[1]

Characters

Dad   -   "Giver"
Mom   -   "Receiver"
Children -   "Predestined for Purpose"

<u>Scene I – Any Home U.S.A.</u>

"The Family the World's Way"

Dad   Lena I'm home woman, what's for dinner?!!

---

[1] The title and the principles of this skit derived from a biblical series taught by Rev. Charles Phillips in 1996

Mom	Well honey I just got home from work myself, and I haven't had a chance to cook yet...
Dad	Yelling loudly, What? You mean to tell me that I've been out on the streets all day long looking for jobs and hanging out with the 'fellas', and I can't even come home and get a decent meal from you, you 'old no count woman!' that I just happen to be married to!
Mom	George, please don't be upset with me because I've had a rough day too and...
Dad	Shut up!! I don't care 'nothin' about your day, all I want is some food and by the way, <u>give me some more money</u> to go out with tomorrow! I'll buy me some more liquor and buy my own food since you're so trifling and won't cook!
Children	Running into the living room "Hi Daddy!" They try to give daddy a hug.
Dad	While brushing the children off Dad yells get off of me you little crumb crushers! If it weren't for you all, I might have done something with my life! All you all do is eat up all of the food, and cost me money, and

God Has Brought Us From A Mighty Long Way!   25

	for what? You kids ain't ever gonna amount to anything anyway!
Finale	Mom and children walk off of the stage very sadly, heads hung down, and tears in their eyes.

Scene II – Any Home U.S.A.

"The Family God's Way"

Dad	Lena I'm home honey, how was your day baby?
Mom	Well George it wasn't too bad at all, my boss was very pleased with that project that I just finished and he is talking about giving me a raise! God is so awesome isn't He? But how did your day go honey?
Dad	Congratulations baby! You are so very right about the fact that God is good all of the time. Well it seems that we've gotten a double blessing today, because old man Taylor called me into his office today! He said he had observed that I was a Godly man and that I always practice my faith

	no matter what happens at work. He said that I was dependable and trustworthy so he is considering me for being promoted to the "Foreman's" position that's open out in the machine shop! And Lena baby you know that will mean a lot more income for our household right?
Mom	Oh George! That's great news honey. Sit down and let me get your newspaper. I'll finish dinner O.K.? And after the children go to bed tonight, we can have our own <u>"special little celebration all right?"</u> She <u>sashays</u> away while smiling.
Dad	That sounds mighty good to me honey!
Children	Running into the living room Daddy, Daddy You're home! They hug daddy's legs and he picks them up and swings them around in a circle like an airplane.
Dad	How are my babies doing today, and how was school?
Children	Daughter Tammy smiling says well daddy I got an "A" in math today and my teacher gave me a reward!

Dad	That's just wonderful baby girl! I'm so proud of you and I know you'll grow up to be the purpose-filled, Godly, and intelligent Christian young woman that God created you to be honey.
	Son Tommy hanging down his head sadly says Dad I had a little bit of trouble passing my spelling test at school today. I only got a 65 on it and I'm so sorry Dad.
Dad	That's not too bad son, we can work on your spelling together, let's pray and ask God to grant you His supernatural favor in this specific subject O.K.? And then we can study together, until you get the hang of it. I know for a fact son that God has a special purpose for your life, so you've just got to hang on in there and keep trying to do your best all right? Tommy looks up and smiles at his Dad while he gives Dad a big hug!
Finale	Dad we love it when you are home, because you make things so much better for us, and Mommy always smiles a lot! The children begin giggling while Dad and Mom hug them both.

The Women's Retreat

Scene I

Church Friends Talking About the Upcoming Women's Retreat

Characters
- "I'm Every Woman!"
- "The Nubian Queen!"
- "Sister You Go! Girl"

I'm Every Woman	Nubian Queen girl! Have you heard about the topic of this year's women's retreat??
Nubian Queen	No I haven't girl! What is the topic?
I'm Every Woman	It's called _"Women of Destiny Destined to Win"_ honey! And girlfriend since I'm Every Woman, and God's all in me, you know that I've just got to be there for this one honey child!

Nubian Queen	Well I'm Every Woman girl I sure didn't hear about this, but I'm so glad that you told me about it, because I love that theme. I know we're going to pick up on a lot of useful and Godly knowledge at this retreat. I'd like to learn more about how to become a more obedient and purpose-driven Afro-centric Queen for the Kingdom of God you know what I mean? And I know that obedience and purpose will be addressed by our speakers with a theme like that! Girl have you mentioned this to "Sister You Go! Girl yet?"
I'm Every Woman	No I haven't yet Nubian Queen, so let's call her over here right now so that we can pull her coat and give her the 411! (smiles)
Nubian Queen	Hi there "You go! Girl" what's going on baby girl, come on over here so that we can bring you up to date on the exciting

happenings taking place at this year's women's retreat!

You Go! Girl

Oh yeah, what's up my sisters?

Nubian Queen

Girl! I just heard that the theme for this year's women's retreat is "Women of Destiny Destined to Win"!!

And everybody knows how you got the nickname "You go! Girl" right? Because you are always utilizing the gifts and talents that God has given you. And whatever you put your hands to do, it always seems to benefit the Kingdom of God girl! Your "attitude of gratitude" always blesses your church family and your natural family. So I just know that you won't want to miss this retreat right?

You Go! Girl

You've got that right my sisters. I try to make it my business to always be available for God's work and to sacrifice whatever is needed in order for His Kingdom building. I know that is the only reason I am blessed and successful today, I give Him all of the Glory and the Honor! I know I can grow all the more at a retreat with this topic. Thank you both for letting me know now because this gives me plenty of time to start scheduling my leave time from work, and for planning my finances in order to go! I surely wouldn't want to miss these powerful messages.

Finale

We're Godly women, bound to be blessed, because we're only willing to give God our very, very best!

Giving God all of the Glory, Honor, and Praise! - 10-09-96

Hallelujah Jesus Found Me!

I thank God for His Son Jesus Christ, coming into my life and saving me at age 37. I also thank Him for giving me answers to questions left unanswered for such a very long time. Prior to coming to know the Lord for myself in personal relationship, not too much in life made any sense to me.

First of all, God had to deliver me from my own self-destructive learned behaviors and habits that I had acquired during the emotionally and psychologically painful progression of my life. The Lord began the process of cleaning me up (sanctification) and healing me (restoration) so that I could and would be fit for use in the building of His Kingdom. You see beloved, God already knows our future before we arrive here on this earth, so from the time of my salvation on I've been working on how to become more obedient in every area of my life. Sanctification is not an instantaneous process, and we all need to acknowledge that fact. We were born in sin, and from that time on we had become very good at "sinning" until <u>TRUE</u> Salvation took place. It usually takes most of us some time to totally yield our will to God's Will for our lives. God made it very clear to me that one of the main things that He wanted me to do was to use my own personal testimony as a tool to reach out and evangelize others. He showed me the errors of my past and made it plain that I had to go out to the highways and byways that God had snatched me off of, to proclaim to this lost and dying world that Jesus is the one and only true and living Son of God and our Savior. God also, instructed me to teach and to preach that He alone has the <u>only</u> real <u>and truthful</u> answers to any and all of the problems and/or questions that we may have in our lives!

Saints of God, all people need to be in a personal and intimate relationship with Jesus Christ. We also need to learn how to allow God's Holy Spirit to live and flow inside of us to guide and direct our paths by opening the doors to direct and personal communication with our Heavenly Father through prayer.

In the first segment of this book called *"<u>From Revolution to Revelation</u>"* You probably were able to identify the various phases and stages that me and many of the brothers and sisters of my generation had to go through as we developed and grew into adulthood.

Later in life we had to be transformed by God into the mature people of God that He would be able to use in this world that we now live in. I pray that God will give you the same kind of zeal that He has imparted to me to reach out to those around you who are still searching for answers in a world full of deceit, darkness, and lies. If you make yourself available, then God through you can direct them to the _True Light_ of Salvation through Jesus Christ the same way that He used others to lead us to Salvation! My prayer is that something from our people's history and the injustices from our past, will reach out and touch your heart, to motivate you to bring the people who are in your circle of influence to a victorious future of eternal life through Salvation in the love of Jesus Christ.

December 31, 1996

WORK SHEET

What does it Mean to Be Saved?
"The Roman Road"

Scriptural references for you to look up and my interpretation of them from the book of Romans (The Roman Road)

ROMANS	Interpretation
3:23	Gives us the reasons we all need salvation
5:12	Shows that we are all descendents of Adam therefore we all must die one day. Death did not exist before Adam's initial sin. So we all are, by heritage, inherently born in sin. Example: When children are born they automatically know how to do wrong things, i.e., pulling things off of the coffee table, learning to say "no" to parents, etc. But children need to be taught what is right.
5:19	Proof text as to how we gained a sinful nature from Adam, and how we later were given access to righteousness through Jesus Christ our Savior.

Romans	<u>Interpretation</u>
6:23	Tells us the ultimate result of remaining in sin and that is death! "The lust of the flesh brings forth sin and sin when it is finished brings forth death."
10:9-10	The simple formula for salvation! All we need to do to receive the <u>gift</u> of salvation is confess with our mouths and believe in our hearts that Jesus Christ is the Son of God and that He died for our sin, ask God to take complete control of our minds and our hearts, so that we may enjoy eternal life with Him! The only way to get to heaven is through God's only Son <u>Jesus Christ</u>. And we all know that gifts are free. But remember, our salvation is free, but it definitely was not cheap!

The Journey Was Not Even About Us

Proverbs 3:5-8 – New Living Translation: "Trust in the Lord with all your heart, do not depend on your own understanding. Seek His will in all you do, and He will show you which path to take. Don't be impressed with your own wisdom. Instead, fear the Lord and turn away from evil. Then you will have healing for your body and strength for your bones."

Acts 1:8 – New Living Translation: "But you will receive power when the Holy Spirit comes upon you and you will be my witnesses telling people about me everywhere-in Jerusalem, throughout Judea, in Samaria, and to the ends of the earth."

Looking Back

When I take a look back on the beginning of my life's journey, I have a tendency to want to analyze it all, perhaps to find some deeper meaning at a more spiritual and revelatory level. Well one of the first things that I asked myself since I am now a more mature and seasoned believer, and also as a student of God's Word, what was it that God was trying to keep me still long enough to see? And more importantly, what was it that God was preparing me to do for Kingdom building.

In the first chapter of this book "From Revolution to Revelation" you took a journey with me through the trials and the tribulations of a generation of young African Americans who were trying to find our purpose and identity during a turbulent and sometimes violent era in our nation's history, and within our own culture and communities. It is my belief that during that time when I didn't even have a clue about Salvation or for that matter anything else spiritual, that the Lord was letting me see a clear and realistic view of the nature of what I can only call the "inhumanity of humankind" and the world that we all live in. I believe that the Lord chose to allow me to experience some of the things that I went through in order for me to realize what it would truly be like to be without Him once I got saved! I always ask God even today, "Lord please don't ever let me get Amnesia?" Because I never want to forget how far He had to bring me from in order to save me Hallelujah!

I'm not saying that you have to experience everything wrong in this world in order to effectively address the world's and/or people's problems and/or issues, but I am saying that what you do experience for yourself in your life makes a much more memorable and lasting impression on you, and those impressions eventually become a very real part of the developing and shaping of your spiritual and your human characteristics. In other words experiences play a big part in who it is that we eventually actually become in our lives.

Make no mistake about it my brothers and sisters, what the enemy Satan schemes, plots and plans for our lives is in <u>direct opposition</u> to what God has designed and predestined for our lives. And it is at this place where many of us can, and sometimes do go wrong. We can fall into the traps set for each one of us by the enemy! It is only by the Grace, love, and mercy of God that any of us reach the place in our lives where we know we need Jesus Christ and allow Him to take control of our lives. Sadly though, many people have totally rejected this awesome gift from God and, thereby, they miss out on God's greatest gift the sacrifice of His Only Son Jesus Christ. The bible makes it clear that by rejecting Jesus Christ they are also rejecting their only chance for eternal life with God and they are condemning themselves to eternal damnation.

I believe that the results of my various early personal experiences and the fact that I got saved, shaped me into becoming a much more perceptive, intuitive, stronger, concerned, caring, responsive, and responsible human being.

It is a known fact that the Lord uses our lives so that once we receive "<u>true Revelation</u>" about who God really is; and what His "Plan of Salvation" really means to all of humanity, we will never turn back or let go of Him and His truths. The sacrifice that Jesus Christ so willingly made for us is the most important truth that the world will ever receive. Jesus Christ is the <u>only way</u> that we can be reunited with our Creator and Heavenly Father God.

Before the foundations of the earth were laid, God already knew who would and who would not accept His gift of Salvation. So my question to anyone who may be reading this book and who has not accepted Jesus Christ as your Savior is, dear ones "what on earth are you waiting for?" The evidence of the love of Christ is all around you, and yet you still hesitate. There are Saints of God around you right now who would be more than happy to show you from the word of God in the Book of Romans Chapter 10:9-10 how to be sure of your own personal Salvation! I once heard it said that "late obedience is still disobedience", I also heard a story about a man who decided to wait until the 13th hour for his Salvation, but he died at 12 o'clock! The bible clearly states <u>"who would neglect so great a salvation?"</u> Please my brothers and my sisters don't let that be your story. God loves you and so do we who are the members of Christ's Body.

You see before God even created me, He knew the passion that He had placed in my spirit to share the good news of The Gospel of Jesus Christ with others! And as we read and study scripture we understand just how absolutely essential it is to God for us to <u>"Pass on to others the truth of "The Gospel of Jesus Christ"</u>

every opportunity that we get!" Believe me Saints of God, there is no other task or mission in the Church that is more important to God than reaching the lost for Jesus Christ! We must never get so busy with "church work" that we forget the true "work of the Church", and that is winning souls to Christ. The bible also tells us "He that winneth souls is wise."

In case no one has ever told you this, let me be the first, "God wants to use you!" Our God is the God of decency and order, so we must never think of ourselves as insignificant, worthless, useless, hopeless, or as failures. God has already equipped you in some way, to be an effective witness for Him. He has given you all of the tools that you need to get started; all you need to do in order to start is have a willing heart and mind. Start by studying God's Holy Word, praying, and listening for that "still small voice in your heart" when God's Holy Spirit is speaking into your life. Be certain that whatever it is that God is calling you to do is "really what God wants" and not a self-motivated or hidden desire that you may have. Because just like the physical laws of our world if we begin operating in the wrong vehicle or switch to the wrong lane, just like in traffic accidents, we will crash and/or sometimes burn out!

You see what many of us fail to realize is that the enemy cannot stop you from Salvation once you've been saved, but his next move is to keep you still and ineffective so that you won't effect anybody else's life for Christ and Kingdom building. So don't you make the mistake of thinking that just because you are saved now, Satan will just say to you Oh well! I lost another one to Jesus, so you go on and have a nice life now O.K.? No, no, no my brothers and my sisters! The enemy will never give up on his plans to trip or flip us up. And that is why it is imperative that we stay prayed up! And ask God for the gift of "Discerning of Spirits." And when we are talking to God in prayer try to remember to make some quiet time so that we can truly hear God's answers to our prayers above all of the noise, clutter, and distractions in our lives and in this world we live in.

In actuality beloved, each and every one of us is made in God's image. We are wondrous creatures that are the Crowning Glory of all things that God has ever created! God has placed us a little lower than the "angels" according to scripture. I once heard a preacher reason that the interpretation of that scripture actually says that God made us a little lower than Elohim, which is a Hebrew name for God Himself, and that the interpreters of the scripture were so amazed at the fact that God would place us just beneath Himself that it was almost beyond their comprehension to even entertain that thought. So instead they interpreted the scripture to say that God had made us a "little lower than the angels". In my opinion, that revelation and interpretation of God's Word is not entirely impossible. We certainly see in scripture that the possibility exists.

There are several biblical and logical considerations of this: First of all, God made us in <u>His</u> own image, secondly because He loved us so much that <u>He</u> sacrificed <u>His</u> <u>Only Son Jesus Christ</u> in order to save <u>us</u> from our sin, and thirdly, throughout scripture God usually dispatches <u>His</u> <u>angels</u> as messengers to us, or to protect us, to rescue us in our time of need, and/or to fight our battles for us. God constantly reminds us that because we are <u>His children</u> we have <u>His unconditional</u> (Agapé Love Hallelujah!) I have never seen or heard of any scripture where God instructs mankind to serve, protect, or worship His angels.

<u>Bringing it all Together</u>

In retrospect I can certainly see how God's plan has worked in my life for His Glory and I can assure you that He wants to do the same for you. First of all, let me say that nothing that happens to a child of God is by chance! All of the tragedies, heartaches, and pains that you have suffered and come through have made you stronger in the Lord and more dependent upon His Word when seeking answers. When you look at your life as a whole, and if you are honest with yourself, you'll admit that if it had not been for the Lord who was on your side, you probably wouldn't even be alive today. So once you've acknowledged these facts you must begin to focus on the events of your life in a different and more meaningful way.

You have to realize and understand that everything that was difficult for you to get through should no longer be seen through "your eyes" as tragedies. You must look at these events and circumstances of life as though you were looking at them through the eyes of Jesus Himself. Because when we look at life through the eyes of Jesus, we realize that we also have the ability to see other people the same way that Jesus saw us when we were so desperately in need! Through the eyes of Jesus, we will have the ability to look beyond other people's faults and shortcomings and begin to see them at the point of their need. As you grow and begin to glow with the love of Christ, you will become more and more "Christ-centered" and less and less "self-centered". Many of us have not risen to that standard of Christ's love in our walk yet. And I must say right here that in order for the "Body of Christ" ("The Church") to function the way God created it to function, we must become more like Jesus Christ! The bible tells us that we are predestined to "conform to the image of God's Son who is our Savior, Jesus Christ."

What Happens to One of Us Effects Us All

When we really and truly empathize with one another as brothers and sisters in Christ, we should automatically genuinely be there for each other in times of rejoicing and in times of sorrow. We should no longer be able to see or think of one another in the same light as we did when we were out in the world. If we are truly blood washed, born-again Believers, we should only act with biblical principles and solutions. Now I'm not saying that we always hit the mark, none of us living in these bodies of flesh will always do what is right. But we must make every effort to do whatever it takes to stand with our brothers and sisters who are members of His Body! In other words, let's keep on "pressing toward the mark of the high calling in Christ Jesus." So even if we miss the mark, we'll still be in the proper arena, and that is among other Believers!

The evidence of our lifestyles and how we treat one another will be one of the most effective ways in which we'll be able to reach those who are still lost in darkness and who are not members of the Body of Christ when we interact with them on a daily basis.

There is one thing that I have learned that I'd like to share right here beloved. No, the journey was not even about us, but how we live is a much more powerful testimony than anything that we will ever be able to say to anyone. Believe me Saints of God, the world is watching us. And when the world watches they are not looking at us from the vantage point of having the ability to discern the difference between what is truth and righteousness and/or what is false and unrighteousness. Remember the same darkness we lived in until Salvation took place, is the same darkness others are living in right now without Christ in their lives. In the same way that we used to be, they are spiritually blind, they have spiritual mufflers on their ears, and they will die in that darkness without our witness! We must remember at all times that as we walk in the victories that God has given us it is essential to share those victories with others. You see Saints, there may be someone watching you who has or maybe is going through some of, if not all of, the same things that the Lord has given you the victory in, and they are desperately looking for answers. If not us beloved, then who will be a witness for the Lord!

<u>Singular Cases in Point</u>

After my son passed away in 1997, every time I turned around God was sending mothers across my path that were grieving over the loss of a child. The first time that it happened was a true set up by God Himself. I had just picked up my granddaughter from her babysitter, and I was backing out of a parking space and had a very slight fender bender with a woman that I did not see driving behind me. No serious damage had been done to Mary's car just a little wrinkle in the bumper. I got out and so did she, I told her that I was sorry and that we should exchange information so that her car could be fixed. Well while I was talking with her she looked so sad, I said to her "you know sweetheart, no matter what happens to us, God is still good and Jesus will always love us right?" Then the Holy Spirit prompted me to remind her that Jesus said in the Word "that He would never leave us nor forsake us." And at those very words, she laid her head on my shoulder and began to cry her heart out. Mary and I sat down on the steps of that building we were in front of and she revealed her entire heartbreaking story to me and how it was affecting her.

God had blessed me with an opportunity first of all to be quiet and listen to someone who was in need. And as it turned out, she had just come from a doctor's appointment in that building after getting a check up, because she was getting over a miscarriage. Although, she had other children this sweet sister (who later became my spiritual daughter) was torn apart at the loss of her son, she had carried the baby for seven months. She confirmed that she was a born-again believer and as she wept in my arms like a child, I was able to console her with my own personal testimony about how God carried me through the pain of losing my own son.

Later on getting back to the "fender bender" that started the entire encounter, as it turned out her husband was a cab driver who had friends who were body and fender repair people. Mary and her husband would not even allow me to pay for the damage. Her family was from Nigeria and they became one of the first of many "spiritually adopted" families that God has blessed me to become a part of over many years (smiles). The works of the Lord in our lives can be so wonderfully awesome when we allow Him to rule, reign, and abide in our hearts. And that was only the beginning of the ministry to grieving parents (though not an officially designated church ministry) that God wanted me to work in. None were more dramatically presented to me than that, but the opportunities continued to flow my way. So you see my brothers and my sisters, as I told you earlier, it wasn't even about me!

Many times believers feel as if they cannot do the work of the Lord unless they are deacons, deaconesses, licensed and/or ordained, ministers, or appointed as ministry heads by our Pastors. But sometimes I believe that many in the congregation become confused about the necessary formalities of ministry. Of course, the organizational structure of a Church is proper and most certainly it is necessary. As I mentioned before our God operates in decency and order. But what I want to mention right here and now is that much of the work of the Church, I would almost dare say most of the work of the Church is done by ordinary people, just like you and me.

I believe that all you need in order to fulfill God's purpose in your life is a willing heart, mind, and spirit and the desire to act upon what He needs from you. Beloved, never forget the fact that there is something <u>special that God has placed inside of you that *only you* can accomplish and/or birth into this earth</u>. No matter what or how things may look to you and your five senses right now. Remember what we see, feel, taste, hear, or think, are not the conclusion of the matter

God Has Brought Us From A Mighty Long Way!   49

when it comes to God's plans and purposes for your life! Just as the bible instructs us to do we must walk by faith and not by sight! Obeying God's voice to serve Him is your first step to becoming a "Kingdom Builder!"

Sometimes a discussion arises and the subject is about how to deal with negative people. You know the people who always want to speak negatively about everything and everybody around them. They seem to thrive on gossiping and tearing someone or something down. First of all beloved, steer clear of any person that constantly displays that kind of spirit and negative mentality. These people are on what I call a part of the "Destruction Crew" because they definitely are not on the "Construction Crew", because we know that construction is the process of building up and not tearing down" So my brothers and my sisters honestly ask yourselves this question, "which crew am I going to be on? Will I be on "God's Construction Crew" or the "devil's Destruction Crew?" And we all know the correct answer to that one right?

What Will Your Legacy Be?

As we grow in the Lord and become more Christ-centered, the benefits of it all will go far beyond what we can see in our lifetimes. Whether we are parents or not, we have to be aware of the fact that the next generation of God's leaders are being directly influenced by us, our obedience to God, or the lack thereof. The bible tells us to "train a child up in the way that he should go and he will not stray far from it" right?

Therefore, I think this is a great time for us to focus on the word "train." The English Thesaurus defines the word "train" as follows:

- Teach
- Coach
- Educate
- Instruct
- Guide
- Prepare
- Tutor
- School

And after researching the word train, I thought that it was very interesting that God chose to use that word when instructing us about how to relate to our children and grand children. If you will notice, every one of the words listed above is verbs. We cannot be lazy and irresponsible with the awesome gift "our children," that God has blessed us with, and the responsibility that comes with training and nurturing them. It takes energy, action, self-discipline, integrity, sacrifice, ingenuity, creativity, dependability, consistency, and genuine love and concern in order to live and teach the Word of God and righteous living to our children. That is the only way they will believe what we are training them for. Shaping children's minds and helping them to develop spiritually, mentally, and emotionally is one of the most challenging jobs that anyone can or ever will have! This Section of this book is entitled "What Will Your Legacy Be?"

In considering that question, I think we all should reflect inwardly and ask ourselves have I been displaying characteristics and a lifestyle that is pleasing to God before my children? Seriously speaking, I believe that some of us are either wavering and/or failing in that area of our lives. Parenting is a daunting task, especially when you have two working parents, which out of necessity is the way most households operate in today's world.

It is my belief that the most valuable gift that you can give your children is your time. If you don't spend enough time with your children you won't even know who they are. Also, we know that most children present themselves to their parents, but they are themselves with their peers. So many times the children that you see in your home, are not who your children may be in other places when you are not around! I used to show up in my own children's class rooms, baseball games, camps, whatever they were involved in unannounced. So they never knew when mom was going to show up, they just knew that I would show up. That little method worked well for me and my family. But as I said above creativity is a key element in keeping things interesting to your young people. So now we are asking ourselves, just how do we teach our children about holy and Godly living in the ungodly environments that they sometimes find themselves in, i.e., schools, extra curricular activities (sports, music lessons, dance classes, science clubs, math clubs), in the homes of other families (some of whom are not Christians), etc.?

I believe that God entrusted us with these precious children so that we can be their heroes, mentors, examples, and protectors of the values that we begin teaching them from infancy. If sound biblical foundations are laid out and enforced in the children's homes from early childhood, it will be a lot easier for them to recognize and say no to things that are not of God. They also need to see the consistency of prayer, worship, and service to God at work in our lives. They need to know what you are watching on TV or DVDs or listening to on CDs and the radio. They need to know that in their home certain ungodly behavior is not tolerated deliberately. The children need to see their fathers and mothers stand up for the Gospel of Jesus Christ at all times without compromising with friends or other family members.

In that way, the children will learn to trust your words from witnessing your actions when you tell them what to do. They will realize at an early age that God cannot and has not failed mom, dad, grand mom, or grand dad, so I know that He won't fail me. And as they grow older and more of the challenges and distractions of life come their way, they will have basic and foundational Godly wisdom far beyond their years, because of the legacy that you built for them when you followed God's Word and "trained them up in His Word while they were still in their formative years (ages 2-12) at home." Hallelujah!

Now I know that many of us did not come to the Lord ourselves until we were older and our children were half or already fully grown up. But that is all right, because you can begin to build a legacy at any age. A legacy is what your children, and their children, and their children's children and other people's children will remember about you and your life lived for God. The impact that your life will make on their lives will be a tremendous one. The benefits of your legacy will depend totally on your choices and decisions. You can either help them live healthy, Godly, prosperous, and productive lives; or without your legacy for God, they can live unhealthy (spiritually, mentally, physically, and emotionally), ungodly, poverty stricken, needy lives that will always be full of lack! And we know that is not the legacy God intends for you to leave.

So beloved, we must re-examine our ways, thought processes, routines, and our busy schedules, I know that if we do that and are honest and unselfish with our self-evaluations we will all be able to find some room for improvement that will make our legacy to our children and our service to God more pleasing to Him.

Love is an Action Word

Once we examine our legacies and decide what it is that we want to be remembered for that will impact future generations, we will realize that every godly action that we take must be the result of our love for others. You see my brothers and sisters, just as I mentioned earlier in this book, we cannot afford to be self-centered in this brief life of ours. We must be unselfish in all that we say, think, or do. Of course, we cannot live our entire lives specifically for other people, but we can discipline ourselves to think differently than we have in the past.

Most of us grew up to believe that self-sufficiency was the most important characteristic to develop as we matured. But after maturing and experiencing all that life can and does throw our way, we began to realize that we needed resources far beyond what we inherently possessed. This is what made us begin our search for the Lord and that is also what will motivate us to reach out to others. If we truly have the Spirit of Christ living on the inside of us, we will care about other people. Whether they are in or outside of our families, whether they live in America, China, Europe, Africa, South America or anywhere else on this earth, we will begin to genuinely care about others.

No beloved I am not proposing that we can solve the problems of the entire planet. I would not be so naïve as to even suggest that you carry that heavy load. But what I am proposing is that we begin to see other people's needs the way that God's sees them. God looks down upon all who are a part of His creation, with caring, loving, patient, and forgiving ways. Remember once again that God wants us to realize that those who are weakest are of the most concern to Him. He doesn't strengthen us so that we can get back on our feet and go on our merry way to do whatever we please. No my brothers and sisters, when God brings us through He has great expectations of us.

We have already discussed how sharing our testimony with others can help them go through trials and tribulations, but there are other things that God expects from us as members of His family.

There will be times when we need to not only say "I love you" but show it with our substance and sustenance. Learn how to sacrifice for others. Learn to share your gifts and talents with others so that they can learn, grow, and achieve more. Decide to dedicate a certain amount of time from your busy schedule to devote to helping less fortunate people who are all around us. For instance, when the "Missions Ministry" in your church goes out to feed the homeless, set aside a certain amount of time that you can and will participate in this effort on a consistent basis. Or in another instance you could join hands with the "Evangelism Ministry" in your church when they go out and about to pass out tracks and to minister to a lost and dying world. You could plan to go with the "Sick and Visitation Ministry" at your church showing love to our brothers and sisters in Christ who are ill or recovering from surgery. Another area you could spread the love of Christ in is with the "Nursing Home Ministry" at your church when we provide love, encouragement, God's Word and other services to those who can longer come out to a church. The "Youth Ministries" in most churches are in dire need of good Godly people to set an example for our youngsters. There are no shortages when it comes to areas in which you can function as a true servant of the Lord serving in humility and love!

Other ways in which you can show love are, we could decide to set aside a few dollars a day for others in need. With what you spend each day on a cup of coffee could be enough to help a struggling family feed their children, or to send one of their children to college. These are small sacrifices that you can easily make beyond your consistent "tithes and offerings." There is so much need in our world, and there are many, many ways in which we can choose to reach out in love and help that would not in any way alter the quality of our own family's lives other than to make them better.

Beloved Beware! Don't Allow Amnesia to Set In

I always remind myself as I'm praying "Lord please don't allow me to lose my faculties of thought processing and memory." We must never forget where God has brought us from. We must never be so heavenly minded that we become no earthly good. Don't settle into a "comfort zone" saints, because as long as we are on this earth, the Lord needs to use us to accomplish His will on earth and for His Glory. I know that the temptation to become lackadaisical is always there. After all, we all lead active and busy lives. Some have busier lives than others, because they have to deal with the responsibilities that come with parenting young children. Others because they have the responsibility of parenting their own parents (care givers). We all have responsibility of some sort. And there always seems to be somebody depending on us. But at the end of all that is said or done, we must never lose sight of who our Lord is to us, and what He needs and wants from us while we're on this earth!

We have a wonderful Pastor and First Lady at "The Sanctuary at Kingdom Square" which is my home church. The Maclins' are classic models of how to handle many tasks at one time without losing sight of who it is that we serve. We should take heed to their examples and emulate them. We want to be more like Jesus, but He needs us to serve Him right here and right now on this earth. We are, after all, "Ambassadors for Christ."

My sincere prayer is that something in this book that will inspire and motivate you to come up higher in your walk with the Lord and in His service. I pray that you'll be able to identify some of the spiritual gifts that the Lord has placed inside of you while you were yet in your mother's womb. And once, you have identified your gifts, my prayer is that you will have enough of the love of God and His Son Christ in you to step on out in faith and use those gifts to encourage God's people and to reach the lost. Once you make a decision to become a kingdom builder, you will experience the greatest joy and peace of your sanctified life. Remember we were all "Broken Jars" but God the Potter can still use us to build His kingdom and to do His will. In that way my beloved brothers and sisters you will truly be glorifying our Heavenly Father.

The bible clearly tells us to be "doers of the Word and not just hearers only."

When people used to tell me that I needed to compile some of my writings into a book, I heard them and hesitated. As a result, it took me far too long to act upon what the Lord wanted me to do. I could probably be on my 10th book by now. So beloved don't you be guilty of the same thing. Once again, there is that saying "late obedience can still be disobedience!"

Besides you might as well obey God right now, because God will have His way and He always wins! Be strong and courageous my brothers and sisters and just like the Nike tennis shoe commercials claim "just do it!"

May the Spirit of God continue to bless and motivate every person who reads this Book I.

Written with compassion for the Body of Christ and in the love of Jesus Christ...our Savior...God Bless Each One of You...

Phase - II - Book Two

"Chronicles of Faith"

Foreword

He has done great things for me, whereof I am glad! *Chronicles of Faith* is a heartwarming testimony of the faithfulness of God. In the midst of trials and disappointments, God's faithfulness will prevail. Even when we do not see the good in our situations, God is ever faithful to see that all things work together for our good.

Through repeated attacks by the enemy of our soul, Minister Harriet was strengthened by the Word of God to withstand and walk in victory. God has already given us the victory in all things through Christ Jesus. To put that victory to work in our lives, however, we must learn to consistently say what the Word of God says, and stand in faith according to His promises.

I am happy to offer Minister Harriet's testimony as a word of encouragement of the faithfulness and goodness of God. I pray that you will take what she shares to heart and act upon it.

Francina Kerr, Th.D
New Directions Ministries

Acknowledgements

First, I want to thank God for giving me clarity of purpose and the vision that it took for me to write this book. I want to sincerely thank all of those who have covered me and this project in prayer. I especially thank God for my loving daughter and friend Jeanna Robinson who has always been the most encouraging and motivating person in my life. I also thank the Lord for my son Don R. Hatcher, Jr. whom I have watched become a gentle and loving man, good father, and who always has loving words expressing his gratitude for having a mother who loves the Lord and people. I also thank God for my wonderful, loving, and dear mother, Nellie Spinner who has since this book's inception gone home to be with the Lord. At a very early age my mother instilled within me that "never give up and never quit" mentality and attitude that I now possess.

I want express my heartfelt thanks to Dr. Franicina Kerr for taking to task, without a moment of hesitation, the writing of the Foreword of this book, and also for her encouraging words and her obvious love for all members of the Body of Christ.

At the time I wrote this book I was a member of a wonderful Word teaching church, Kingdom Christian

Center Church International (K.C.C.C.I.) in Washington, D.C. where Dr. Charles Phillips is the Visionary. I will always be grateful for Dr. Phillip's teachings on faith, wisdom, and tenacity especially concerning the things of God.

God has since ordered my steps and directed me to my present church, The Sanctuary at Kingdom Square, in Capitol Heights, MD, and I am under the spiritual authority of the awesome Visionary of that house, Pastor Anthony G. Maclin, who is the most anointed, Christ-centered, encouraging, empowering, and motivating man of God that I have ever known. I truly appreciate Pastor Maclin's example of leadership and dedication to the things of God and His people. If it were not for his sense of urgency, I may never have gotten around to publishing this book. Pastor Maclin makes certain that the members of his congregation know that we all have important and various gifts that can be used to contribute to the building of God's Kingdom. I also want to thank our First Lady, the awesome woman of God, Minister Peggy D. Maclin. Minister Peggy who is the Director of our Watchcare Ministry (which is for membership retention), the President of the "Daughters of the Kingdom Women's Ministry", and who is a great example of a "Godly Woman." Her lifestyle has truly effected my life by showing me how to strive for excellence in all that I do. The Maclins are wonderful leaders of a family-oriented church and I thank God for them both.

There will always be an "attitude of gratitude" as I humbly accept the assignments and tasks that God gives to me for Kingdom-building purposes. There is nothing quite as humbling as realizing that God turned what used to be a "wretch like me" around, and that He wants to use me as I live my life to fulfill the purpose and potential that God had in mind when He created me.

       Minister Harriet Edmondson – Author

Introduction

"Chronicles of Faith" - is a testimony of a three-year period in the history of one Christian woman's faith walk with God in which she came out victoriously simply by believing and confessing the Word of God and His promises.

First, I want to say that this book is not intended as advice, counseling, or a guide to anyone else about how to conduct his/her own personal walk with the Lord. This book is just a personal testimony concerning the goodness of God, and a word of encouragement to anyone needing one. This book speaks of the faithfulness of God and how He has blessed my family and me. It is my sincere hope that this book will help the "Saints of God" remember what our Grandmother's used to say to us honey just "Hold on to God's Unchanging Hand" until the manifestation of your own personal victory comes to pass.

<u>Hebrews 11:6</u>

"But without faith it is impossible to please Him: for he that cometh to God must believe that He is, and that He is a rewarder of them that diligently seek Him."

Simply put, this is a chronicle (*or record*) of the faith that it has taken for <u>me</u> to live as "more than a Conqueror through Him that loves me." This record only covers the trials and the victories that God gave me over Satan during a three-year period (1996 through 1999).

I believe that the miracles and victories that God blesses us with need to be made known unto all men and, <u>especially</u> to other Christians who just might need a word of encouragement in some of the same areas of life in which you've already been tested and have come out of successfully. The Holy Spirit confronted me with this question, "what better way to reach people than through a book?" I obeyed Him and this book is the result of my obedience. I pray that this book will be a blessing to you and your loved ones.

The chronological order of these events started in October 1996, which is the year that I began to experience intensified attacks from the enemy in every area of my life.

First Wave Assault – Physical Attack

Exodus 15:26

"And said, if thou will diligently hearken to the voice of the Lord thy God, and wilt do that which is right in His sight, and wilt give ear to His commandments, and keep all His statutes, I will put none of these diseases upon thee, which I have brought upon the Egyptians: for I am the Lord that healeth thee."

During a routine physical examination, my doctors discovered that one of my vital organs was malfunctioning. Then after further testing and examination to confirm the problem, I was told that medical science had no cure for my ailment. Well my mind immediately went to a valuable lesson that I'd learned long before this happened. I was told by a Pastor that doctors only have the letters M.D. behind their names because they stand for the words "medical degree" which means that they have a degree of knowledge about medicine! In other words they do not know it all when it comes to God's creations.

That valuable lesson reminded me of the fact that Almighty God, who is my creator, who knows everything about me; and who possesses "Limitless" power would never have a problem fixing anything that is broken or malfunctioning in all of His creation. Therefore, I had no doubt that God would not have a problem healing me, His child, no matter what the doctors were saying. In other words Brothers and Sisters, I had to hold on to what the Word of God said about me for my healing. Now let me say this, I did follow my doctor's advice.

On top of all this negative news about my health, very soon afterward I also lost my job! And in today's world no job not only means no money but also no health insurance.

Well the doctor prescribed and stressed the importance of taking specific medication for my condition and he told me that I needed to begin taking it as soon as possible. The next challenge that I had to face was the statistical history of the medication I had to take. I was informed of the fact that only 33% of the people taking this drug had responded favorably to it, and that only 1 in 5 African Americans responded to this medication at all! Then the doctors told me about the <u>possible side effects</u> of this drug, i.e., high blood pressure, severe joint pain, skin rashes, diabetes, depression, etc. etc. Well! After hearing all of that I asked myself the question, why would I want to take a medicine that could be so potentially harmful? After all I did not feel sick from this condition at the time, so I began reasoning why should I take something that might make me feel

God Has Brought Us From A Mighty Long Way! 73

and/or be sick? I had no medical insurance to pay for this very expensive medication and I wasn't even sure if I wanted to chance taking it. At that point I decided to do what I believe all believers should do, and that is continue trusting God and praising Him for His faithfulness! Every day during my prayer time I made it my business to plead the Blood of Jesus Christ against every Satanic attack that came my way. Meanwhile, I just continued focusing on living the life that God had already blessed me with.

I'd like to insert a note of <u>caution</u> here, because if you're not very careful, Satan will very subtly and almost imperceptibly attack your mind and your spirit at times like this with his demonic influences of <u>fear</u> and <u>denial</u>.

If you don't maintain a strong prayer life, you could begin to rationalize in your own mind by thinking "I don't need to be listening to these doctors anyway?" You may even begin thinking, after all, I know Doctor Jesus and it is by His stripes that we are healed right? Yes, that is true Saints, but we also need to acknowledge that God has also given us the wisdom we need to determine and seek the good things that He has provided for us in order to take good care of our health and bodies. The same way that wisdom dictates that we should watch what we eat and drink, or how much we need to exercise our bodies in order to enjoy excellent health.

<u>All</u> knowledge comes from God; therefore, all of the medicines and treatments that the doctors prescribe for us are tools that the Lord can and will use to help us at the greatest time of our need. Medicines have <u>therapeutic value</u>, but God is the one who actually provides us with <u>our healing</u>! If we don't remain spiritually alert, the enemy will attempt to delay our medical treatments with vain rationalizations. Delays in treatment in situations like the one I was in could have allowed the enemy enough time to intensify his attack on my body. We must not fall into the dual traps of <u>fear and denial</u> Saints of God.

Of course, we must always pray and seek God's face, but we also need to do what the doctors advise us to do. We must remember that generally doctors are not our enemies so we need to follow their advice. But because of my jobless situation, more than a year actually passed before I got the treatment that I needed. All the while the Holy Spirit led me to continue speaking the Word of God over my own life and circumstances. So I just kept on placing my absolute trust in God's Word. And I believed Him for my own physical healing. I rejoice because our Lord is so gracious and merciful. During that time of inescapable delay God did, in fact, protect me and He kept my condition from worsening.

When God blessed me with a new job and health insurance, I was finally able to obtain medical treatment. This was only one of many ways in which

God Has Brought Us From A Mighty Long Way! 75

God was showing me just how much He cares for us His children. Let me remind you to always remember to focus on, to cherish, and to value God's love for you as an individual.

God is constantly showing us His faithfulness, and sometimes Brothers and Sisters; we fail to even acknowledge His goodness. Often times we get so busy with life that we ignore the fact that we need to maintain our efforts to grow in His grace. Never stop developing your relationship with God through prayer, fasting, and the study of His Holy Word.

Another point that I would like to make is that God will use whomever He wants to use in order to get His blessings to us. A case in point is that God used a clinical nurse that I had never met before to bless me. I met her at the hospital clinic during a visit, and she intervened on my behalf by calling a particular pharmaceutical company in California to inquire about a study program that she had heard about known as the "Commitment to Care Program." She wanted to determine my eligibility for this prescription program, and sure enough I was eligible for it! Hallelujah! God is so loving and <u>faithful</u> to His children. The Lord does not want us to be encumbered with worry or distress in any situation.

The only thing that our heavenly Father wants any of us to do is obey, worship, praise Him, and to proclaim

His goodness throughout the world while we walk in absolute Victory!

The fact that God provided a way for me to get this medication without having to pay for it truly was a miracle Saints. This particular medication had to be taken for more than a year and it ended up costing from $250-$500 every two weeks. Later on during my treatment the medications changed and cost $2,500 a month. Then there was an additional medication I needed that cost $500 per month! So you see beloved, what God in His <u>faithfulness</u> did for me was not a small thing, but rather a <u>major blessing</u>! How excellent is the name of the Lord! We know for a fact, that God takes care of His own all we need to do is <u>call on Him</u> and to <u>trust in Him</u>. (Hallelujah!)

I would also like to remind you that the manner in which we go through trials is just as important as getting through them. We must be mindful not to fall into the trap of the "spirit of <u>grumbling and complaining.</u>" After all, we know that the Hebrew people did a lot of "grumbling and complaining" while in the wilderness and that spirit caused them to wander in the wilderness for forty years instead of completing their journey in what could have been approximately 3 weeks. We must remember to thank the Lord always that things are as good as they are no matter what our five senses tell us; because the bible tells us that we are already blessed and also that "the battle is not even ours it is the Lords." And I don't know about you,

God Has Brought Us From A Mighty Long Way!   77

but knowing that I'm in a battle and I'm on God's side of it is very comforting to me because God never loses!

Meanwhile, during my visits to the clinic and doctors offices I always deliberately maintained a Spirit of praise to God, lifting up the name of Jesus every opportunity that I had to do so. During various blood tests and other procedures, I would tell the technicians that I was looking forward to a praise report from God! Sometimes they looked at me like I was crazy, but that never stopped me from proclaiming His Word. I spoke of the Lord's goodness to staff, nurses, doctors, other patients just everyone I could talk to. I passed out Daily Bread booklets, bible tracts, etc. even to the security staff outside of the clinic. And anytime I actually had the time to have a conversation with others, especially other patients I told them about God's miraculous healing power and about His goodness and mercy toward us. The Holy Spirit revealed to me, during this time that we should never allow ourselves to become so distracted by our circumstances or situations that we forget to praise the God of our salvation or pass up an opportunity to lift Him up.

We must also remember our vows to God, especially during troubled times. The Holy Spirit let me know the importance of being about "my heavenly Father's business" during this time (without excuse). Therefore, I obeyed Him and continued to serve the Lord not only at church, but also in the Ministry God had given me to serve in called "The Hour of Love Service" held monthly at the "Northwest Healthcare Center Nursing Home" in Washington, D.C. I kept on sharing the good news on my job and in my neighborhood too. But, the most important revelation that came to me during this trying time was to remind everyone that we must <u>never</u> abandon our relationship with God, no matter what else may happen. After all, He is our <u>only hope</u>! Hallelujah!

By the way, not only was the medication I received free to me, but remember those potential side effects that the doctors listed for me earlier in this testimony, well in my prayers I asked God to not allow those side effects to come upon me. And once again, God showed me His faithfulness, because I only experienced minimal side effects from the medicine. It never came to a point where I was unable to function on a daily basis. The doctors were truly astounded by this, because their experience was that nearly everybody who had taken this medication had suffered so badly from the side effects that they could no longer function normally or work while they were taking it. But great was God's <u>faithfulness</u> to me! Hallelujah!

During that time another very valuable lesson that I was being taught is that we need to be specific in our prayers. We must know what it is that we want from God, and not be ambiguous about what we want from Him. When it comes to His children, God leaves no stone unturned. He cares about every single thing that concerns us. Also, we need to learn how to pray the way that the Bible tells us to pray in certain circumstances.

Let me share with you the specific prayer that I prayed during this ordeal and how God answered my prayers. I said "Lord I want the laboratory tests and the results from the tests to line up in agreement with Your Word." I know that in _Isaiah 53:5_ you have told us that Jesus was "wounded for our transgressions, bruised for our iniquities, that the chastisement of our peace was upon Him and that by His stripes we are healed."

This is how God responded to that prayer, at the beginning of this medical challenge I was given a test. The test was an indicator of how much damage had been done to my body and the numbered results were relatively high (660,000). After I prayed the same test was repeated and I was informed by my doctors that the resulting number was so low that the laboratory could not even assign a number to it! Just look at God, He always shows up and He always shows off His awesome power when we need Him the most! Hallelujah! The doctors were and still are baffled (smiles) they said that there was only a very slight indication that my vital organ even still had the problem that they had previously diagnosed! They admitted that they could not figure out what had happened, but believe me I knew, it was by His stripes I was healed! I truly give God all of the glory, honor, and praise that are due to Him! And let me inform you that any bible scholar will tell you that <u>all</u> absolute science aligns itself properly with God's Word. This was truly a miracle taking place in my life and body for the entire world to witness. Again, God was showing me <u>His faithfulness</u>! Remember Brothers and Sisters, He can and will do the same for you if you just continue to "<u>walk by faith and not by sight!</u>"

<u>Proof Text</u>

<u>Psalms 118:17</u>
"I shall not die, but live, and declare the works of the Lord."

Beloved, I am here to tell you this day that I am walking in Divine health, long life, and the joyful strength of the Lord God Almighty!

<u>Hebrews 11:1</u>
"Now faith is the substance of things hoped for, the evidence of things not seen".

We serve an awesome God and He has imparted His power and anointing to us through His Son Jesus Christ our Savior. But if we don't know about the power that we possess or how to use it, we might as well not even have it.

And that is why it is of the utmost importance for us to study God's Word, to continue learning from those spiritual leaders that God has placed over us and in our lives, and to remember who the *"Author and finisher of our faith"* really is. God alone has the final say in our lives. He is our Creator and He is concerned about everything in His creation. Remember: God cannot lie nor can He fail!

__Second Wave Assault - Emotional__

__Psalms 29:11__
"The Lord will give strength unto His people; and the Lord will bless His people with peace."

Before I get into this next testimony, let me say that as a Minister of God's Word, I personally believe that God hates divorce. We know that marriage is representative of Christ's relationship to the church. Jesus Christ is the bride groom and the church is His bride awaiting His return. Therefore, my sincere prayer is that anyone who is married will do any and everything that he/she can possibly do to preserve his/her marriage. The following is only an individual account of my personal path __down the aisles__ of matrimony.

First and foremost, let me say that I could have avoided living through the following ordeal if I had only waited on God to send me the husband that He intended for my life. But I didn't, once again I got ahead of God. The result of my own personal ignorance and disobedience to God back then had far-reaching and serious consequences.

God Has Brought Us From A Mighty Long Way!   83

God sent four people along before I got married to warn me about the impending matrimony. But in my mind I failed to acknowledge that God had sent these messengers, and that they were only expressing their opinions. In hindsight, I now realize that I should have taken heed and waited, but I didn't.

At that time I was quite immature spiritually. Let me say that I was not a member of K.C.C.C.I. at that time, because K.C.C.C.I. is where I ended up being taught the value of being sensitive to the leading and guidance of God's Holy Spirit, and about obeying Him. During this marriage, I was at the first church that I attended which was a church that taught a lot of God's Word, but they did not teach or stress the importance of the operation of the Holy Spirit in the life of a believer. As a result, I knew very little about the gifts of the Spirit or what they meant in a Christian person's life. I guess you could say that I was spiritually ignorant. I ended up paying a high price for that ignorance and the bible clearly teaches us the following: *Hosea 4:6* *"but my people are destroyed from lack of knowledge"*.

Well, going through the challenges of my marriage turned out to be a very humbling experience for me, and God used this experience as a tremendous life-lesson to me. In my opinion, God used this marriage to teach me to always wait on Him (something that many of us don't like to do) and to be obedient to Him concerning all of life's decisions. But more than that,

God has shown me that He has to be <u>first</u> in my heart in order for me to be able to experience really <u>true love</u> with anyone else.

The Lord also revealed to me that He sometimes will allow us to go through trial and error in order to teach us how to live righteously, so that we may teach others how to do the same. You see, eventually we become more mature and seasoned Saints that know how to walk in total obedience and victory; by paying attention to and by studying God's Word.

In February 1997 the man I was married to and I went through a separation. By the way, this was not something that took place suddenly, but rather it was the end of a nineteen-year journey. Please be mindful that these time frames are not meant to imply any set framework for how God will work in your lives. God deals with each one of us individually, because He loves us just that much.

During this ordeal, I had to repeatedly make a conscious decision to stand in <u>faith</u> and to personally walk according to the Will and the Word of God. There were times when that was not an easy thing to do. There were many emotional and psychological distractions that tried to take me off my course, and I found that I had to be very careful not to let that happen. At this point, the enemy was attempting to use all of his tools to <u>"shake my faith."</u> Instead I found out that no matter what happened or what I experienced, God's love for me was strong enough for (His and my) relationship to remain intact, therefore, I was able to endure. God would not allow anything to "<u>shake my faith</u>" for God is always faithful and I was operating and functioning in <u>His strength</u>.

I will say this, that separation does hurt, but I was not <u>bitter and defeated</u> because of it. It is very important beloved, not to allow feelings of bitterness, failure, defeat, or rejection to settle in your heart when you are going through emotional upheavals. The reason I can honestly say this is that by this time I had truly repented for making one of life's <u>most important decisions (MARRIAGE)</u> outside of God's Will.

In one sermon I heard a very renowned Pastor say *"True repentance comes from a change of mind, a change of heart, a change or actions, and finally a change of conduct."* I totally agree with that preacher, repentance does not mean just telling God "I'm sorry," but it does require that there be genuine change from within.

Another thing that I had to be careful of, I could not afford to allow the enemy to pull me into what I call the *"blame game."* When we are in the midst of emotional turmoil, it is always easier to blame someone else for our troubles. But I believe that as Christian adults we should remember that whenever we decide to do anything outside of God's Will, it is already bound to fail from the outset. Also, being completely honest with yourself always helps. Because that is when we understand that any <u>final</u> decisions we have made in our lives were ours alone to make. In the end, it doesn't even matter what influences we were under; we had choices and we made them. So we need to learn to live with that fact and take appropriate action, or in some cases inaction, as required. Like any good father our heavenly Father chastises us in order to correct us and help us to grow. The *"blame game"* will cause you to waste a lot of unnecessary time and mental energies.

Well after much prayer, seeking answers for my life in God's Word, and by totally yielding my spirit to God's Holy Spirit, the Lord reassured me that I had done all that I could do to keep this marriage together. At that point in the relationship, I was certain that God had released me from the bondage that is the result of being "unequally yoked" in marriage.

You see Saints, God <u>can fix any mess in our lives</u>, but He certainly is not <u>required</u> to fix <u>every mess that we make in our lives</u>! That is when God's grace and mercy steps in! Thank you Jesus! Once we know God's Word, it is our responsibility to obey it and to apply it to our lives.

This is how the Holy Spirit led me through this separation and eventually divorce (in 1999) while maintaining my peace of mind and strength. I intentionally focused on God's unconditional and personal love for me. Then in time, it became easier for me to move away from the pain and disappointments of my past and to look forward to a brighter future. Again I thank God for <u>His</u> <u>faithfulness</u>.

Brothers and Sisters there is no pain or problem that is too difficult for God to deliver us from it. I am now in total peace and living with no residual feelings of bitterness or anger that could hinder me from effectively doing the work of the Lord.

To anyone who is in a similar situation, all I can say is that only God can and will bring you through such painful and stressful times, and He will bring you out with a total and complete sense of wholeness, healing, purpose, and victory.

We must always remember that no matter how difficult things may seem, we <u>must</u> yield our will to God's Will for us. When we do this, God will continue to use our testimonies to glorify Himself in all of the earth. We must learn to walk in what I once heard called "sweat-less victory." Amen!

Third Wave Assault - The Family

Psalm 1:1
"Blessed is the man that walketh not in the counsel of the ungodly, nor standeth in the way of sinners, nor sitteth in the seat of the scornful."

My mother had a major stroke in March of 1997, and the doctors told me to prepare for the worse, because most likely she wouldn't live. But as a believer, I refused to agree with those doctors or their prognosis of mother's condition.

The above-referenced scripture let's us know that we are not to agree with people who are not in relationship with God, and those who do not seek His counsel. So I held on to my <u>faith</u> and I continued to confess God's Word over my mama while she was being healed. As you read earlier in this book, I already knew first hand from my own miracle of healing about God's healing power.

Now since the devil couldn't get me to confess and agree with that first lie that he had used the unsuspecting doctors to tell me, he decided to try another lie (after all he is the father of all lies

God Has Brought Us From A Mighty Long Way!   89

right?). So the doctors said, "well even if your mother lives, she will never be able to walk or to talk again!"

Once more, I had to tell the doctors that I respected their opinions, but that is all that they were *"their opinions"* based upon their limited knowledge. So I told the doctor "there are two things that you don't know sir, you don't know my God and you don't know my mother!" I simply told him and his colleagues that my mother had already been healed by God. They looked at me in a strange and patronizing way, and they told me that they understood. I knew from their responses to me that they had decided that I was a religious person who was in denial about the reality of mother's situation. But Saints let me make something clear about people who are unsaved and not in a personal relationship with our Lord and Savior Jesus Christ, they simply are unable to understand or even comprehend the comfort and privilege that we have as children of God. So we can't expect them to agree with us either. Just make sure that you know <u>who you are</u> and more importantly, <u>whose you are</u> when you believe God for miracles, whether the need is for yourself or for your loved ones.

Now let's examine what else God did on this <u>faith walk</u> of mine. Three weeks after all of those dire predictions and the hopeless prognosis made by her doctors, my mother and I <u>walked</u> out of that hospital together and not only was she <u>walking</u>, she was <u>talking</u> and giving me orders about which door to pick her up at! (smiles) And I was more than elated to be hearing those orders coming from the mouth of my sweet mother.

Hallelujah Saints, I want you to be reassured that <u>yes</u> we can believe God for our loved ones, even when they cannot do it for themselves. My mother's healing was <u>total</u> and <u>complete</u> with no visible or invisible signs of her ever having had a stroke. Mother made a 100% recovery from that stroke.

Now Brothers and Sisters isn't it just like God to bless us with the cake and then He puts the icing on it later? You see, prior to that stroke my mother was not saved, but after her recovery from the stroke she got saved, and became a born-again believer who grew in God's grace for six more years. She was a member in good standing at a powerful church in our hometown of Baltimore, Maryland, Huber Memorial U.C.C. where the awesome Pastor P.M. Smith, presides and nurtures his flock, and where the Word of God is delivered in a powerfully life-changing and dynamic way all of the time.

Mother grew in God's grace and in the knowledge of His Word at Huber, and she became an active member of the "Champions of Faith" ministry visiting and caring for the sick and shut-in and all of this took place when she was 74 years old (Hallelujah)! Beloved, don't ever stop praying for your loved ones, as I've been saying throughout this book <u>"Great is His faithfulness"</u> our job is to stay focused on His promises and to pray through until we receive a break through! Amen

Fourth Wave Assault – Attack On My Very Soul

1 Corinthians 15:20-24 (N.I.V.)
"But Christ has indeed been raised from the dead, the first fruits of those who have fallen asleep. For since death came through a man, the resurrection of the dead comes also through a man. For as in <u>Adam all die, so in Christ all will be made alive</u>. But each in his own turn: Christ, the first fruits; then when He comes, those who belong to Him."

When my youngest son passed away on April 22, 1997, the enemy had taken his "best shot" at me. More than anything, I can say that this is when "the rubber met the road for me! If my love for Jesus and my faith in God had ever been put to test, it was during this time. You see, before I became a believer, my children were my life to me! There was no doubt in anyone's mind that my children were my only real reason for living. Back then, my love for my children was greater than for anyone or anything else (including myself). Because in spite of whatever hardships we went through, I hung on to my children with all of my might. Being the very young single mother of three I always tried to keep our parent-child bond secure. Although difficult at times, I embraced the job of mothering with all of my heart, using everything that I knew about being a good parent to my children, and trying to learn anything that I could to become even better at it. The children were very young when their father chose not to remain with us.

Yet, never in my wildest dreams or imaginings did I ever expect one of my precious children to leave this earth and go home to be with the Lord before me! No parent ever expects that to happen. But, as it happened my thirty-year old baby boy died.

As laypeople, we often think of hospitals as non-threatening safe havens. It is practically a foregone conclusion in our minds that we as Christians should always pray for and visit our loved ones when they are hospitalized. But may I encourage you right here and now to make sure that your presence is known, seen, and heard to the hospital staff whenever someone that you love is hospitalized.

Our family prayed for my son Glen, his sister Jeanna and I even kept an all night prayer vigil over Glen during a previous illness that he had been hospitalized for.

Well picture this, the hospitalization in which my son died happened during the exact same time that my mother had been hospitalized with a paralyzing major stroke. And because she was unable to move or talk, I decided that I needed to stay with her (at age 74) practically all day and night. But I maintained contact by phone with Glen (he was hospitalized with a high fever from an unknown source at age 30) needless to say, I could not be in two places at one time. In my mind it was more important to stay with the elder and more critically ill loved one. And you know from a previous chapter in this book that my 74 year old mother made a 100% recovery but my 30 year old son died!

What made the situation more painful was that the hospital in which Glen was a patient did not even give us basic human respect. First of all, the hospital waited twenty-eight hours to even notify me that my son had died. They claimed that they could not find my phone number. Also, before they notified me of his death they had already performed an autopsy. The legal loophole that the hospital created in order to do an autopsy without family's consent was that they declared that Glen had died under suspicious circumstances in their hospital. In Maryland that automatically gave them the right to perform the autopsy. Later we discovered that because the hospital did not initially know what had caused Glen's death, i.e., <u>whether they were at fault or not,</u> they had attempted to cover up the true circumstances surrounding his death with a contrived web of lies and deception. That hospital's lack of compassion, concern, and consideration made the experience and pain of losing my child almost unbearable.[2]

The coroner's report stated that my son died from the <u>onset</u> of a previously undetected[3] heart condition called "acute myocarditis" which in laymen's terms means that he had inflammation in his heart muscle and fluid had built up around his heart causing him to have a fatal seizure because of the pressure from the fluid on his heart.

The only thing that I will say here is that God is still <u>faithful</u> because my baby Glen was a <u>born-again believer</u>. He had accepted Jesus Christ as his Savior and was baptized at the age of sixteen, and at the age of twenty-seven he had recommitted his life to the Lord. I am comforted knowing that he and I will be together once again in heaven. God's comforting Word clearly states that "My grace is sufficient unto thee...".

Although that hospital operated in a totally disrespectful and harsh manner toward our family, as Christians, we knew that we could not allow ourselves to harbor any feelings of hatred or vengeance towards those involved. The hospital was not my real enemy,

---

[2] That particular hospital in Baltimore is no longer in existence. Several years after Glen's death, it was demolished and where it used to stand is now a parking lot.

[3] If the hospital Glen was in for 3 weeks had been thorough, they could have detected this condition before it worsened.

but I know who is and so do you. His name is Satan referred to in scripture as the "evil one." God is the only righteous judge and during our grief and healing process my family and I have prayed for all person(s) whose actions or lack thereof in any way may have contributed to Glen's death or who may have added to our grief, pain, and suffering.

So once again Satan tried, unsuccessfully to separate me from the love of God. But instead, I can honestly say that my love for God has increased. God comforted me in ways beyond mere human explanation, during a time in my life where events occurred that was emotionally very traumatic and that could have been devastating for me.

But because of <u>God's faithfulness</u>, my relationship with Him is stronger than ever before. Be sure you remember that there are times in our lives when we will have to totally depend on the Holy Spirit to carry us through, and this ordeal was definitely such a time for me. As I've said before and I will continue to say "<u>God is always faithful.</u>" No matter how much pain we sometimes must bear, remember He has promised "never to leave us nor forsake us."

According to the bible, Satan's only purpose is to steal, kill, and destroy. Therefore, the fact that he hates and wants to kill the children of God should come as no real surprise to us. Now in the midst of this painful ordeal, the biblical knowledge that I've incorporated into my life enabled me to continue walking in my God-given victory, yet not destroying my testimony as a witness for the goodness of Jesus Christ.

God, in all of His infinite wisdom, grace, and mercy literally surrounded me with His love and comfort as He led me through that tragic time. Let me say that we also need the love of God to be manifested through His people at times like this. My natural family and my church family at that time truly came through for me. I will forever be grateful for the tremendous outpouring of love and concern that was shown during this painful time for me and my family.

There is one thing that I often hear people erroneously say, when they are confronted with the loss of a loved one. They will say "why did God cause my loved one to die?" Beloved please do not get the blessings of God and the evil works of Satan confused. Because the bible tells us clearly that God is "<u>The Creator</u>" and the <u>source of all life</u>. The bible also clearly describes Satan's works as that of a <u>thief, a killer, and a destroyer</u>. God is our Healer and our Deliverer! Satan is the cause of sickness, death, and destruction! We must never let our emotions cloud our judgment.

Whenever you want to realize how intensely God loves us, just remember that He gave His only begotten

Son, Jesus Christ just to save us all from the power of death, Hell, and the grave!

As a mother and a human being, I can't and I don't think I ever will be able to say that I am over the pain of losing a child. Because I will always grieve for and miss my precious son's physical presence more than mere words could ever express. But those emotions could never stop me from loving and serving my God. As a matter of fact, after Glen went home to be with the Lord, I became all the more determined to serve God. My lifelong goal is to remain committed to reaching the lost for Jesus Christ.

Book II - Conclusion

In conclusion let me say, that in every way and even under the severest attacks, I have experienced the presence, comfort, and the victory of God in my life.

My dear Brothers and Sisters in Christ, we must hold fast to our <u>faith in God</u>, to the power He has given us as His children and joint heirs with His Son Jesus Christ, the power and protection of the cross, and the precious blood of <u>Jesus Christ</u>!

Stand firm on the biblical truths that you know, and know that God's Holy Spirit will intercede for you even when you feel powerless, or think that you cannot make it through! Have faith, trust God even when you can't trace Him. And never forget, that no matter what you may see, hear, think, or feel in the natural realm, just keep on believing God in your own spirit and then thank Him for <u>your own victorious walk of faith</u>!

I often find comfort remembering the words of this old hymn that my grandmother used to sing to us: "<u>It is no secret, what God can do, what He's done for others He'll do for you...</u>"

Most of all my Brothers and Sisters, please understand from this personal testimony of mine, that no matter what you are going through, God <u>will</u> <u>carry</u> <u>you</u> <u>through</u> it all, He <u>will</u> <u>be</u> <u>with</u> <u>you</u> <u>always</u>, because "<u>God is Always Faithful!</u>" If you would sit down one day, and begin to make a list of all of the blessings that you have already received from God, I'm sure that you will run out of paper and have to start a new list sooner than you could ever have suspected. When you get finished making your prayer journal, you'll see that you have your own personal *"Chronicles of Faith"* I guarantee you that it will bless you and those who are around you, because your testimonies will be an encouragement for others who are or may be going through some of the same things that God has already taken you through.

Now may God continue to bless and keep you…and…May His Holy Spirit continue to lead, guide, and direct your paths according to His Will.

October 1999

Printed in the United States
83445LV00003B/195/A